The History of M

A long time ago, before money was invented, pe[...] things they needed.

That means they traded for things—just like in the lunchroom! While you might trade your chips for someone else's cookies, the first barter probably involved trading animal skins for food.

Bartering worked great for a long time, but it had its drawbacks. First, there was the problem of hauling around loads of animal skins whenever you went shopping.

1

Then, there was the "what equals what" problem. (How many animal skins equal how much food, anyway?)

Finally, there was the "what if you don't want what I have to trade" problem. (What if I want to trade my animal skins for your food, but you don't want them?)

Clearly, something had to be done to make trading easier. That's why the first money was invented.

The First Money

In the U.S., Native American tribes used colored beads and polished shells for money. They called this money *wampum*. In other places around the world, people used animal teeth, stones, cocoa beans, feathers, and many other unusual things for money.

Salt was used for money in some parts of the world. It was considered valuable because it preserved and flavored food. But there was one serious problem with using salt as money—it melted whenever it got wet!

Using Metal for Money

Someone finally came up with the idea of using *metal* for money. Bars made out of metal were easy to carry. And everyone could agree on what they were worth. But it wasn't long before people realized that sometimes they needed to make change. So, small pieces of metal—"coins"—were invented.

Coins first appeared in the land we now know as Turkey. The first coins were very beautiful. They were made out of gold and silver, and were stamped with the image of a lion's head. Some of these coins are more than 2,500 years old. They can be seen in museums and private collections.

When people in other countries saw the first coins, they thought they were a good idea. So they began making coins too.

Using Paper for Money

The Chinese were the first people to make paper and to print on paper. They used hand-carved wooden blocks to print their money. This was much easier than making money out of metal. Eventually, the idea of paper money caught on everywhere.

The History of Money in the United States

When the American colonists declared their independence from England in 1776, they had no money to finance the Revolutionary War. So the Continental Congress began printing money called "Continental Notes." These notes were used to pay the army and to buy supplies for the troops.

In 1787, the first U.S. coin was minted. It was a copper one-cent piece. On one side, the words "WE ARE ONE" were stamped. On the other side, the words "MIND YOUR BUSINESS" were stamped.

This coin was decorated with 13 linked circles. These circles represented the 13 colonies that had fought for their independence.

In 1791, the Continental Congress decided that our money should be called "dollars." This is because Spanish *dollars* were used in the colonies at that time.

Many Types of Money

In the early days of this country, each colony printed its own money. Even cities and private businesses printed their own money.

All the money looked different, and sometimes stores would not take the type of money people wanted to spend.

This confusion lasted until the Civil War in the 1860s. Then President Abraham Lincoln signed a law that made U.S. dollars the standard currency for the entire country.

"Green Backs" refers to the ink color on the back of dollars issued in 1861 to finance the Union war effort.

The Federal Reserve System Is Created

The Federal Reserve System has three divisions—12 regional Federal Reserve banks, the Board of Governors (in Washington, D.C.), and the Federal Open Market Committee. All three divisions watch and control the economy. They can *raise* interest rates to slow spending and hold back inflation. They can *lower* interest rates to encourage economic growth. And, they can limit the amount of money in circulation.

The Federal Reserve Bank system, created in 1913, is sometimes called "The Banker's Bank." This is because it circulates money to commercial banks—the banks found in your neighborhood and town. Almost every large armored truck you see is either going to or returning from a Federal Reserve Bank.

The Life of a U.S. Dollar

Since 1877, U.S. dollars have been printed in Washington, D.C. by the Bureau of Engraving & Printing—which you can tour if you're ever there.

Obviously, security at this building is tight! There are hundreds of video cameras, thousands of alarms, an army of security officers, and hardly any windows.

New Money

Newly printed money is put into armored trucks in Washington, D.C. and is delivered to the top-security vaults of America's twelve Federal Reserve Banks, located around the country.

The Federal Reserve Banks hold the new currency until local commercial banks request it.

When bank customers cash a check through their banks, they get the newly printed bills.

'Paper' Money Isn't Paper

Although the formula for making dollars is top-secret, the biggest surprise is that "paper" money isn't made out of paper! It's made out of cloth because cloth is stronger than paper. "Paper" money is three-fourths cotton and one-fourth linen. Scraps and cuttings from blue jeans are part of the secret "paper" recipe!

Federal laws control the production of the paper and the secret ink formulas.

Inflation

If you watch the news on TV, you may hear someone talk about "inflation." Inflation means that the price of things is going up.

Let's take bikes as an example to show how inflation works…

If a factory makes a lot of bikes and no one wants to buy them, stores will lower the price of bikes to sell them faster.

But if a lot of people want to buy bikes, stores will increase—"inflate"—the price of bikes. This is because they're more valuable when a lot of people want them.

The same bike that sold for $100 one month might sell for $125 the next month, if a lot of people want to buy bikes.

So, inflation happens when a lot of people with money want to buy a limited number of things.

When inflation happens, your money is worth less because you can't buy as much with it.

Too much inflation in the economy is like too much inflation in a balloon—if something isn't done, it will break! That's why we have the Federal Reserve System with its Board of Governors in Washington, D.C. It can step in and put things back on track by making changes in the economy.

The United States has experienced hardly any inflation in the past several years.

Counterfeit Money & the Secret Service

The Secret Service—those people in suits with dark glasses and earpieces—are best known for protecting the President. But the Secret Service was actually created in 1865 to help stop counterfeiting (making fake money).

Why is counterfeiting so bad? Remember when we talked about how inflation makes the value of money go down? Imagine what would happen if millions of dollars of fake money flooded into the country! Real money would be worthless!

In the U.S., $20 bills are the most counterfeited note. Outside the U.S., $100 bills are the most counterfeited note.

Money with a New Design

To fight counterfeiting, the Bureau of Engraving & Printing recently added new features to our paper money. These features include a security thread, an enlarged, off-center portrait, a watermark, and color-shifting ink.

The $20 bill below shows the new anticounterfeiting features on U.S. bills!

Portrait
The detail of the enlarged portrait is difficult to copy. It is off-center to allow room for the new watermark.

Watermark
Held up to the light, a watermark just like the portrait can be seen from both sides.

Security Thread
A special thread is embedded vertically to the far left of the portrait. The thread glows when it's held under an ultraviolet light.

Color-Shifting Ink
The number in the lower right corner on the front of the bill looks green when it's seen straight on. It appears black when it's seen at an angle.

Different Kinds of Money in the World

Nearly every country in the world has its own official money. About 140 different currencies are used in the world today. These currencies have different histories, names, designs, colors, and values than U.S. money.

Countries exchange currencies so they can buy products from each other. Something called an "exchange rate" lets people know just how many pesos, yen, francs, or marks equal our dollar. Exchange rates can change daily.

Country	Currency	Country	Currency
• China	yuan renminbi	• Japan	yen
• France	franc	• Mexico	peso
• Germany	deutsche mark	• Netherlands	guilder
• India	rupee	• Spain	peseta
• Italy	lira	• United Kingdom	pound sterling

How Does Money Grow?

The best way to see how money grows is to open your own savings account at a bank. Now start saving and see what happens! Let's say that, every week, you put $5 in the bank and your cousin spends $5 on candy.

The money you put in the bank starts growing immediately. This is because banks pay "interest" on money. When the interest is "compounded daily," this means that the bank pays you every day for keeping your money. You're making money by simply leaving it in the bank!

More Money Facts!

$ $ U.S. coins are minted (made) in two U.S. cities—Denver and Philadelphia. (Other U.S. mints produce commemorative coins.) Philadelphia is the world's largest mint. It even produces coins for other countries!

$ $ All U.S. coins have two sayings stamped on them: "E Pluribus Unum" ("Out of many, one") and "In God We Trust."

$ $ Even the U.S. Treasury makes mistakes. The Susan B. Anthony dollar, minted in 1979, was not a popular coin. Americans thought it looked too much like a quarter. So, there are 334 million of these coins in storage.

$ $ If your paper money is torn in half, but there's at least 51% of the bill remaining, a bank will replace your money.

$ $ All U.S. paper money has a portrait on one side, and a building or a monument on the other side.

$ $ The Yap Islanders in the Pacific had stone money that weighed several tons. Some of their large, round stone money was taller than a basketball hoop!

$ $ The average $1 bill lasts about 17 months. Then it has to be pulverized.

$ $ Every day, about $400 million in paper bills is pulverized by Federal Reserve Banks. If you put all the $1 bills that are pulverized each year into a stack, the stack would be 200 miles high!